No Place For Hiding

No Place For Hiding

New Poems by John L'Heureux

DOUBLEDAY & COMPANY, INC., GARDEN CITY, NEW YORK

1971

Poems in this book have appeared in the following publications:
THE SECRET WAR, THE THING ABOUT CATS, RITUAL,
Texas Quarterly, Copyright © 1970 by Texas Quarterly; THE
LETTER, *Motive*, Copyright © 1969 by The Board of Education
of the United Methodist Church; SOME LOGIC FOR MY
BROTHER, G.M.H. and OF VARIOUS CONSTRUCTIONS,
The Month, Copyright © 1968, 1970 by Peter Hebblethwaite,
respectively; THE DAUGHTER OF HER HOUSE, *The Beloit
Poetry Journal*, Copyright © 1970 by the Beloit Poetry Journal;
THE OSTRICH LADY AT SCHOOL, NIGHT LOGIC, THE
REPLY, *New Orleans Review*, Copyright © 1970 by Loyola Uni-
versity, New Orleans; THEFT, EVENING PRAYER, *Spirit*, Copy-
right © 1969, 1970 by Seton Hall University, respectively; CAR-
PENTER, TO HIS SON, *The Catholic World*, Copyright © 1969
by the Missionary Society of St. Paul the Apostle, in the State of
New York; BEING AND BECOMING, EXEGESIS, *The Atlantic*;
FROM ST. IGNATIUS LOYOLA, FOUNDER OF THE JESU-
ITS: HIS AUTOBIOGRAPHY, *New American Review*, #6.

for
MIKE AND CONNIE HASSETT

Contents

IV. *from* ST. IGNATIUS LOYOLA, FOUNDER OF THE JESUITS:
HIS AUTOBIOGRAPHY

[with directions for reading]

V. PRIESTS AND PENITENCE: WARS OF FLESH AND ROSES

Little Wars:
Some Secret, Some Ritual

THE THING ABOUT CATS

Cats hang out with witches quite a lot;
that's not it.

The thing about cats is
they're always looking at you.
Especially when you're asleep.

Some cats pretend they're not looking
until you're not looking.
They are not to be trusted.

Some cats scowl because they're wearing
imitation fur. They feel inferior.

Some other cats look at you straight on
so that you can't drink your drink
or make love
        but keep thinking
that cat's looking at me straight on.

But all cats do the same:
they look at you
              and you look out
and in.

A cat is not a conscience; I'm not
saying that.

What I'm saying is
        why are they looking?

THE LETTER

They found you starved
eating from a bowl
of nuts and bolts
that was your gun
dismantled. Your full eyes
stared the sun down.

Robert, come home.
Leave your tattered grave
and iron worship
to your betters.
We will murder you
decently beneath the trees.

By the moon I see
you are dumb earth
and I cram your mouth
with berries and sick cream.
Come home to your mad
family. You are dead.

THE SECRET WAR

He bought your youth
for that bruised mouth
and exhausted flesh.

No use to argue
with him. He knew
what you had been, valued

what you might
become: his neat
mind shaping your slow wit.

When you drowned
yourself the second
time, he knew he owned

your purchased soul
as well. All
his hopes were full.

He would inscribe,
he thought, the tender lines
of his desire

upon your self.
Not fearing hell,
you let him have his will.

It was then he drowned
himself, seeing he was damned
and you—somehow—had won.

5

NIGHT LOGIC

My pointed paper hat embarrassed me.
I was a salesman selling oranges
at a roadside stand. Ridiculous.

You passed by, laughing, and refused
to buy a nickel orange so I cursed you
seven times, until the small cry
a rabbit makes, shaken by a dog—
instinct teaches how to break a neck—
sliced the night air and I woke
horrified and hating. Someone died.

Asleep once more, I dreamed your burial.
Mourners came in small groups to buy
an orange for your grave. But I
would not sell. I knew what I had done.

THE REPLY

that quick jump
out of time
was your last trick

you held your breath
forever

I had not known
silence
would lie upon your tongue
like a threat

knowledge
was what you wanted
you have it

and I have wisdom
ashes on my lips
grit in my teeth

underneath their pennies
your blind eyes
search my eyes for answer
that I cannot give

I have blown out
both the candles

I will do my own dying

THE THREAT

Because you were my enemy
I loved you

as much as my narrow heart
would tolerate. I hated you

because you knew me.
You hated me because I did not

know you. Somehow we failed
to think of murder. I loved you

grudgingly and you, new Adam,
let yourself be loved. Though

grudgingly. Now you are my brother.
We who could lie dead lie open

to the enemy. Trespass, brothers,
you who dare.

SOME LOGIC FOR MY BROTHER, G.M.H.

Having noted spots in things
reverenced every melted cloud and hillock
sold your soul for bread and a cup of wine

will you pray in the streets
with such a one as me?
(That is, finally, the question.)

I wonder and think yes.
We shall walk in silence for a while
and—after you have drunk your modest wine,
after my immodest several wines—
I shall be patient with your fish and fields and farriers,
you will indulge my Kit Smart's cat
who counteracts the devil
(who is death, who never prays in streets)
by brisking about the life. Thus we shall praise God.

thus beyond the dim mists of logic and of longing
we shall love one another (counteracting death)

and then go back to a land black and white
Jesuits and priests
alone as Cain waking, cold, in the fell empty night.

RITUAL

we have heaped words like stones
you and I
upon the stillborn carcass
we thought we recognized

and still you say more
your grace
your soft eyes gone too adamant
to say it

only to say it
we face each other stones in hand
the small body
forgotten

THE EYES OF MORNING

Better here in white sunlight
in complacent air. Eyes start
at sudden brightness, squint,
contract as the heart contracts
even before it knows. Better
here in the street, in sunlight.

And so you say it. And castles
fall. The imprisoned Prince,
a bastard offspring loosed
upon a hard impartial day, runs
screaming on the battlements
his flaming hair a fallen emblem.

Later, at the curb, the child
will mourn his lost prison.
Better here in white sunlight,
with no sound of grief. Only
the scuffing of our soles, only
a hand raised against the light.

CARNIVAL

It is the logic of your love
defeats me.

When I reach out to touch your arm
and find there
a knot of sinews tightened against my entry
against some sick flower that never bloomed

I am stripped in a seamy carnival
sweating under the lights under the noon glare
under desperate smiling people who point
and nudge and clutch their money
in terror at my shame

and my heart contracts
vomit rises in my throat
because I know it will always be this way.

I do not want to die.
I have no such thoughts.

EYE OF THE NEEDLE

Is anything all right
I ask
and because you are not dumb
you do not answer.

The body is complicated enough,
let alone Greek vases; how
can you explain music neither of us heard?

You wait, silent. Silent,
I grow numb. We become two different ends.

When things are simpler,
next year perhaps,
we could take a course, study language. Together.

Because I am not you. I am not. Help me

help me place your hand upon my heart
or hip
or slick elusive soul.

I am locked in a Grecian vase, smooth,
with music for a shell. Nothing
is right.

Find me   find me

                      answer

CONSOLATIONS OF PHILOSOPHY

Before they cut my uncle up
   to fit him in the box
   they asked permission.
      (consideration fails
      when mostly metaphysical)

My uncle after all was dead,
   had never walked well,
   why fight about a leg?
      (still, death should image
      what our lives should be)

They had uncles too
   and understood our hesitation.
   Well, finally we agreed.
      (moral constancy
      requires gradual repose)

We felt glad we could oblige.
   They cut him up neatly,
   tucked him all around.
      (failure need not be
      the moral constant)

And we said goodbye. We did
   our best, tried to offend
   no one, mostly succeeded.
      (death is final
      and promotes virtue)

The Daughter of Her House

The Daughter of Her House

THE DAUGHTER OF HER HOUSE

1.

She has been hanged and comes back now
for vengeance, I thought. No blood left.
She will brood forever twisted in that chair.

Once she was twenty-two and sang in streets,
read medieval history, walked five miles
each day. She washed in sun and silly lotions
bought for flawless skin. Guaranteed. Her skin,
despite the lotions, bloomed peach and almond
on her fine bones. Only the mind was flawed.

Her dowry was a curse, so Hawthorne said,
standing at the curtain of his Sunday window,
having seen the aunts—the supple aunts
and fathers of Brook Farm—stumble blind
from their Utopia. Weeping for their vision
and their cold gray eyes, he drew the shade.

She brought her dowry and her wide gray eyes—
soft then as deep water, warm with love—brought
her singing and her books and bones, lived
happily ever after. For a year and seven months.

Then the inquisitions started. "The truth.
Do you love me? Or not? I want to know."

"Yes, I love you," he would say and laugh
that she could think herself unloved. Later
he grew tired.
                    "Do you really? I want to know.
I *have* to know."

                    "Oh for God's sake, yes,"
he said, passing his hand before his eyes
where the pain began; and then, "I'm sorry.
Yes, I do." But his heart darkened bit by bit.
She brooded, lonely, certain no one loved her.

Finally, of course, she had her way.
He ceased to love her. Or perhaps
he loved her still but was deprived
the right to give—one cannot give
what is demanded—and gave no more.

Her hard gray eyes grew hot
with madness and she scratched
the almond from her skin
when she awoke
and found him
gone.

2.

In the eighth summer, the year
she strangled on his heart
and died whispering, "Can't it ever
be beautiful? Can't love ever be
beautiful?" he found his mind
had torn down the middle.

He missed his heart, but grieved
for his torn mind. He dreamed
of window shades frequently
and finally when he saw the doctor—
who urged he take a rest and find
a hobby—he knew the shades
were drawn for good and realized
he had died. Death, he had thought,
was more expensive. No matter.

That year he spent by the water.
"Taking the baths," he said to friends,

smiling wryly at the pity of their eyes.
They could not see his heart returning.

The mind came later. He set about
repairs in winter of the second year.
He read some books on art, on love,
on arts of loving, on sex. Sex books
were the best, proposing an aesthetic
of the loins he recognized as funny.
And with laughter came release.

He dated time then from her death.
"It is three years now, years of the Lord,
since the eighth summer," he wrote
on postcards. "Three and a half years.
I am writing an obscene novel." He never
finished. He met the elderly madonna
who rumbled to the waters with sunrise,
back again at night to her parrot
and geranium, and found himself in love.
"But I'm safe. I know that gambit."
He packed and left, returned again
to the uncomplicated warmth of friends
who never risked the word of love, left
him, so he liked to think, free.

His mind is mended now and his heart
is strong enough; it seems to flourish
in our warm wet climate. He thinks
of her rarely: gray eyes devouring
his own, an almond branch in rain,
a young voice singing. But he is free.

"Peace means not to be involved,"
he says. And he is busy. He reads
and keeps up on things in general.

3.

She, in dreams, had wandered in a jungle:
all the flowers folded inward, petals
bending back upon themselves to hide
the groping heart. Leaves of metal clinked
upon the wire stems. Carefully she crushed
the fleshy blossoms in her hand, tore them,
knelt in anger to rip hard roots from earth,

but then the earth exploded and she found
herself trapped among familiar mirrors.
Her face, her haunted eyes, bloomed
like evil plants. Hands, thrown up to shield
her from her eyes, attacked. She ran,
and stumbled on herself.

                Waking, she thought
she saw them at the gate, blind and foolish,
groping from the garden one late fall afternoon.
Smoke was wisping in the leaves, the smell
of burning would remain with her forever.
They turned to watch the fire and she saw
their eyes grow cold; they did not look
at one another. The vision done, she found
she could not weep.

                She strangled finally.
Her blackened lips still formed the "beautiful"
that was her last complaint. Unwilling
to accept the gift with grace, she chose
her self, the holy cell of the determined damned.

In her red wig and willful lovelessness
she sits forever brooding in the antic chair.
Her wide gray eyes look in, appalled, staring.

Prayers and Threats

REGINA

As royalty
of course
we are ridiculous

because though regal you are not arrogant
and I though able do not presume.

Besides, I love you.
Enough to level any kingdom.

Then there are your skirts
halfway to existence
and your stockings smooth as rippled snakes
and your long hair

tangled in my mouth
sometimes   those
times

you are so soft
(I said) and warm
immensely happy (you said) you say

our words become that crazied glass
of a world that shows us
us
(ridiculous, regal)
but breathless anyway and still believing
love survives the folly of our nights.

We are rich enough to pity Caesar.

THE HERETIC

Having exhausted
    snow flakes and the dogwood petals
    I turn to your tongue

drawn deep into my mouth
    with all my body needling, curling
    into yours. And you

not knowing, wondering
    at my mouth. Love is vulgar business.
    But so is living, dying.

Even the Crucifixion
    was flesh; a tongue nailed to the wood
    and love flapping

in the wind like a voice
    never wholly heard. You are a heretic.
    Love begins with bodies.

THE OSTRICH LADY AT SCHOOL

You have said no thank you
to a pearl necklace
to a silver coocoo
to some excellent chablis.
You have declined to talk
with famous men
with beautiful and not stupid women.

You are content
in a condemned slum tenement
with me.
Well, you've had your choice.

When we stepped off the roof last night
and kept walking on the sooty sky
the ostrich lady was looking and looking
her sandy eyes sharpened
for the moment when you hand me back my book
and yawn. You laughed instead.
She slammed her window
though she is said to know a great deal.

We, however, knowing little and not caring,
walked for two hours and twenty-three minutes
before we fell.
The sky gave out and we were talking still.

Regardless of the grammar
we are glad to hear the things we say
those times,
the things we know already.

Listen.
Listen.
She is flapping her reluctant wings.
Tomorrow when we amble through the air
we must talk slowly and be careful
to invite her in the dance. We'll show her how.

Those sandy wings will never bear her up
until she learns to sing no thank you
to a pearl necklace
to a silver coocoo
to some excellent chablis.
With love, all things.

NIGHT LETTER TO REGINA

Theft became a necessary gift.
When I stole the car and drove
off into darkness like a mythic
Jesuit, it was for you. To give
you something poor. You have
rubies, hearts, and poems,

but not a car stolen by a priest
who has to see you or go blind.
It was the fairy at the wedding
did it, lighting cigarettes
and smiling, smiling at me—
the poor priest who does not guess

love's secrets. I do not guess;
I know. It was not me but you
that he blasphemed. Sweet,
I am no mythic Jesuit. I am
the thief they never catch. Yet
I swing nightly on the gallows.

THE FIRE

The house wears a facade of ice this morning.
Fire glowed there seven winter hours, water
turned the iron trees to feathers. I
who have burned to death seven winter times
enjoyed it. It was, in its way, perfection.
Although they broke the windows and the window
frames and chopped the arms from chairs
and broke the crockery, nothing stopped the fire.
The frozen flames unfolded to illumination.
There were wings somewhere and air moved gently
on the stricken night. No one called.

Your letter came at ten o'clock this morning.

EVENING PRAYER

Here I sit, SuperPriest,
(four books published; God!)
and, half drunk on five-dollar scotch
altogether drunk on love for you,
I solemnly proclaim:

had I the tongue of Robert Lowell,
Baby, everybody would flex the old knee
to YOU,
killer diller, the genuwine article;
they would blow their minds.
(You've gotta be contemporary.)

Is that Lazarus I hear snickering?
The old celestial giggle? (Well, hell,
we all deserve a laugh.) And life,
besides,
is Whoozee's Chambered Nautilus
and death is no more scotch
and no more you.
Even Robert's gonna
pack his whaleboats and his cousins
and shag his ass across Nantucket waters.
"Is that a sail I see?"
That's Mister Charon, Baby, bleeding pennies
out of tourists.

Which says—through scotch and loneliness and loss—
wait.
If love survives the passage to the grave, mine will.
This poor priest's will. Oh

wait for me.

THEFT

1.

I lay dead
for fifteen years, you know,
until your heart

beneath my nervous hand
pulsed me back to life.
I wrapped you then

in a brown parcel
and tucked you
in my pocket

and I shall never let you go.
When the police go by
I smile

and they, the law,
smile too
thinking I am merely mad.

But no.
I am alive
with you with you with you.

2.

I wake
in the night
and turn to you

fearing
you will not be there.
You are not there.

I knew it. Stupid
then that I should lie
awake

saying
"my God my God
you can't be serious"

because he isn't.
And that
is always the point.

I wake alone
and no heart now
pulses me to life.

3.

It was after all
a mistake.
That's how things are.

You
can shape darkness
to desire

but I am a poor man
by vow
and talent

and now
I see what you are—
riches—

and I
surviving on a daily gift.
Take this brown parcel:

it is
the only thing I ever feared
to lose.

31

BEING AND BECOMING

I am becoming a ghost if it is possible
to become what I have always been.

I can tell. My arms had drifted off
some weeks ago, three weeks at least,
and my stomach gone for quite a time,
but now, tonight, walking from your house
at two A.M. I felt my feet evaporate
and knew the truth. I am becoming

a ghost. A no-footed haunter. Spooks
will be my intimates, my grim consolers,
and I will find my truest self. Person
to person. But that will have to wait.

Right now I am in process. Once the legs
have gone, the head, the stupid torso,
once the heart has whisked along the street
as soot or ashes or a nuisance in the eye,
I shall desist. I shall be the ghost I am.

But you, alchemist, I shall forget you never.

from St. Ignatius Loyola,
Founder of the Jesuits:
His Autobiography
[with directions for reading]

from ST. IGNATIUS LOYOLA,
FOUNDER OF THE JESUITS:
HIS AUTOBIOGRAPHY
[with directions for reading]

1.

"The Early Years"

Manresa and the mango trees and the sterile landscape
stretching out like an unimaginative hell.
It was a good place to begin. (Beginnings
always look that way, viewed from the end) The cave bit
came much later after whores and horses and a ball
in the knees (for a switch) and some literary quarterlies.
     [he is resigned]
Well, you work with what you've got.

2.

This is a reflection
and you can't expect Palestrina
for Christ's sake
when it's only a priest humming while he scans the landscape
casually on a Saturday afternoon
without even a telescope.

3.

Yes   well   I suppose
it's been a good thirty years—
no acceptance   no warmth   no tenderness   no
(can even a psychiatrist say it seriously,
be serious when he says it?)   no love—
     [he sighs]
a good thirty years for writing and thinking
     [he smiles]

35

and stuff like that.
(It's a tough thing when you're a saint to write
your autobiography)

4.

"The Augustine Syndrome"
    [to be read only while drinking]

You have to smile a little, don't you?
Because it's funny. It is.
    [am I drinking too much?]
I mean we get off the subject quick if it hurts. No one
cares about the great excess; it's the little secret dirt
they want. The slip.
    [he drinks, frowning]
We're all alike and, what the hell, it all . . .
    [he forgets]
it all comes down to the same thing.
You know what I mean? I mean
it's important to be yourself. Your
    [he is drunk]
real
genu-wine (I'm just saying it that way to be funny)
self.
    [he knows what they are thinking]
I mean
    [he goes on anyway]
I mean that's the most important thing.
I mean,
Christ,
if you're not yourself
    [he screws up his face]
what are you?
I mean, really.
But anyway mirrors are very important
in the ultimate scheme of things.
    [he is talking to the mirror]

36

Ultimately, the most important things
are love. I mean that's what they resolve
down to—the important things—love.
And I think that's a very important thing
ultimately.
    [he is lost]
I do. I mean—honest to God, no shit—
what are you, what is anybody
except himself? You know?
Excuse me. I have to go the bathroom.
Even saints have kidneys.

5.

"Alarums and Fanfares for the King's Supper"

Professional help, Cripes, yes!
You've got a clear mind
and a good body
and being a saint wears the hell out of you.
Out of me
is what I mean.
There was this girl,
see,
with long black hair and everything.
(This is complicated, I think)
Well, anyhow, her hair was long and black
and always moving
like a black light or a dark water
or a mind looking and looking
but the thing is it was moving   changing   forming
(on the wind) a new word
to tell me
ask me
what   what
what do you want
what is it
what   what

say it   only say it
then—
you know how it is—
the darkness was too much or something
and I said,
hell,
what about having a peanut butter sandwich
for lunch tomorrow
while she stood there
handing me pieces of her heart she had chunked out
with her thumbnail and—
understandably—
she turned away, sick.
Well hell, yes.
Bring it on. I could use
some professional help.
      [he lapses]
(Move a little and I'll slip it in)

6.

"Conversion"

Up on those goddam battlements with the wind
freezing your ass off, you really wonder about things.
You know you've had it anyway
and you say what the hell, dying's not so bad,
it's living screws you up.
      [he is factual]
Here you are standing around
waiting to make roast beef out of guys
you don't even know well enough to hate. So they play
The Star-Spangled Banner
and baby
you fight to the death
(They say that in the army. I know. I was in the army)
So meanwhile I'm back on the battlements
freezing my etceteras

when this pistol ball comes whizzing around a corner
and takes my kneecap with it.
They find me among the living,
more or less,
and I am here to tell you all today:
    [he proclaims]
support your local draft board in its hour of need.
I did.
My Cardinal, right or wrong.

7.

"Interlude"

Purists get upset now
that I've dropped control: easy fun, they say, but cheap.
Dear Purists, it wasn't easy;
have you ever tried to drop control?
(Drop, I said. I've never lost anything)
it wasn't fun; hop into the showers
at Buchenwald and smile, baby, smile.
(Smiles don't come easy to me. Honest!)
it wasn't cheap; twenty-five bucks an hour
and somebody you'd like to love
treating you like a complicated hernia
(That's the worst part; it's called living)
Dear Purists, get your non-fucking hands off me.
I've earned my dropped control.

8.

"A Philosophical Excursus on 'Gift, Giving, To Give'
According to St. Thomas' *Commentary on the Sentences*"

A real gift is never something that you need
like teeth
or a turkey on Thanskgiving
or a pail of money.

A real gift is when you crawl in through my eyes
    [he speaks in a monotone because this is philosophy]
and sit around for longer than you want
until you forget you're there
and I forget you're there
except sometimes.
A real gift is when that doggy who had everything
sighed and said:
"It's true. I do have everything.
But there must be more to life than just having everything."
You can always tell a real gift
because you know that to keep it you've got to give it away.
(That's how philosophy is; it's difficult)
And so in this, the income tax season, I discover
I have given you seven non-gifts, three partial-gifts,
and now, I think, one gift.
Non-gifts:
    1. my sex life
    2. my intellectual life
    3. my emotional life
    4. my mother
    5. my father
    6. my brother
    7. my hatred, anger, and associated virtues.
Partial-gifts:
    1. the three times we laughed
    2. the love you had already
    3. the weaknesses you had not known about.
One gift:
    1. Some words, these, which no one ever said before—
       not in this order anyway.
Is this a poem? Hell, no. It's reality, a gift.
You can't keep a gift.

"Spiritual Consolations and the Gift of Tears"

Madam, this requires a little explanation.
    [he is patient throughout, almost]
This water I have drawn, painfully,
out of my eyes,
out of my brain,
(a doctor got some out of my spine
with needles and a headache)
out of my heart
(which holds very little blood). I have prepared
this water carefully and, as I said, with pain.
To be honest,
Madam,
I hoped for holy water.
I had planned a pool, perhaps,
or a fountain
(if we can find equipment)
or simply some nice thing. Just a nice good thing.
    [he is almost patient]
And now look.
You've got your beautiful broad-bottomed fat little baby
smack on its ass
in the middle of my water.
    [for a moment he forgets the lady's age and rank]
Lady, take your goddam baby quick.
I want my bath water.
    [he ponders her mystery]
Besides, how'd you ever get a baby without loving?

"Pilgrimage"

Yes   well   I suppose
it's good to be back. Once you've seen Christ's feet
printed deep
in the Rock of the Ascension
you're pretty willing to settle for a Paris grammar school.
    [he—does he sneer?]
(What the hell, it will look romantic in the history books)
And I like kids. They're closer to where
it's at.
If it's at anywhere.
    [he pauses, making everybody get serious]
Christ is.
I'd like that in italics. Because—
there's always a because and it never makes sense—
because it's been hard, damned hard.
Thirty years of pressing my goddam Basque nose
against Parisian bakery shoppes
where they put away the cream at three;
thirty years of coming too late for anything
(so laugh; you've got a dirty mind);
thirty years of trying to say to St. Francis
Ex-say-vee-ur
"Frank, I love you; don't get shook"
and him trembling like some kind of crazy spastic.
    [he reflects]
Maybe we should start a corporation.
Christ!
(Sometimes you can't tell
if they're cursing or blessing)
Stick with me, baby,
and you'll wear mink. Or mourning.
    [he threatens]
Or your face,
your own for once,

42

borne before you like a mask
confusing the hell out of everybody
and when it drops
they'll, all of them, know your absolute control.
    [he wonders]
I never thought you had control
and now I see
    [he smiles]
that was the problem . . . thinking. Excuse me.
The kids have come
and I've lost my place.
    [he is confused]
At first,
when you're first back, everything
is . . .
    [he gropes]
                . . . I almost said
you love me.

Priests and Penitence:
Wars of Flesh and Roses

THE INDICTMENT

When I feel madness coming on
I force myself to think of Boston.
Superiors would never give approval

to hysteria. They deplore it, exhort
their sons: obey. "It seems to us
better that you plan on no hysteria

this month. Or next month. But be sure
you are remembered in our prayers."
God's not on vacation; he's visiting

the missions. So I postpone madness.
Today administers its numb barbiturates;
I concentrate my grinding teeth

on getting through tomorrow. And
I survive. Plunge to my knees each
morning, turn toward Boston, and obey.

When I am dead, I ask you, open
my heart. Teresa's proved she was
a mystic. Mine will prove I had one.

EXEGESIS

All your plants have grown
and flowered and the fruit,
though hard and a little bitter,
has kept you rich.
                    You spend
yourself only on important
enterprises where the profit
will be certain. You have time
for everyone provided he has
reason. You have never been
foolish in love, never failed.
Your orchards thud all summer
with the sound of quinces falling,
your corn is late when prices
are the highest; all your plants
have grown.
                    Dear Brother in Christ,
I am thirty-three and bury you
who are thirty-four because alive
and talking, talking, you are dead.

Your fields are ripe for harvest.

OF VARIOUS CONSTRUCTIONS

This morning while that priest
was hawking revelation to disciples
drawn by incense and the sound
of holy ease, I found my soul.

I had been scooping sand around
my feet when suddenly I touched
a living thing. The talk went on
and no one noticed I had died.

Brown and scrawny, awful tendrils
clotted it and what I had been told
was beautiful lay there ugly,
gasping. I stared in comprehension.

Still, it was my soul—I have lived
with harder truths and reconcile
myself to more—and so I loved it.
That sometimes happens at the beach.

Quickly, to anticipate the second
coming, I packed sand around it,
smoothed and patted the small mound,
blessed it finally, unobserved.

All morning I lay washed in sunlight
staring at the last horizon, talk
and talk behind me as Messiahs
preached their gospels to the poor.

ILLUMINATIONS

The china cats
were what he liked best,
white
and green
and a rather extravagant yellow.
He found it hard
not to be
always praising
since he saw the splendor
everywhere.
And yet he feared that he was damned.

Over scotch
he said,
It's true,
I wake each day
with guilt upon my tongue,
taste it every hour.
I sleep digesting my despair.
He spoke
coldly,
detachment born of too familiar grief.

We left the bar
and walked
along the raining street.
It was then he saw
the china cats.
He stopped,
stood there several minutes.
Look,

he said,
white
and green
and a rather extravagant yellow.
He came away,
damned
but laughing.

All ahead was rain.

ACCIDENT: CHRISTMAS, 11:45 A.M.

The trees have all gone home
and the moon, with no dead
arms to shine through, has lost
its pale and specious mystery.
We could almost laugh at it.

We could almost laugh at it
here together in your car
except there is no moon,
only sun blazing on the snow
like an angry firing glass.

Like an angry firing glass
the sacred oil glistens
on your neck, your ankle
in the noon sun this Christmas.
You lie huddled in my arms.

You lie huddled in my arms
crushed beneath the window's
splintered light. Moon and sun
become one awful broken mystery.
The trees have all gone home.

INCARNATION

Around
and around the grave I walked
and walked for thirty years, impaled
my palms upon the twisted iron spikes,
blood spurting on my clothes, my shredded arms,
and still I could not enter.

They have buried me in there, I said, and waited.

So when your sly tongue created me
out of death
and stark imaginings
I thought you must be mad.
All the others needed flesh.

I watched, fascinated at your method.
Burial, decay, selective resurrection;
and then astound me with my soul.

Later, when my hands were healed,
I went back to the grave, walked past
the iron palings and the spikes, and scratched
the earth away. The bones were soggy
and the gaping skull was spent.
No butterfly ascended from that clay.

I give these bones—
you never needed flesh—
to you.

CARPENTER, TO HIS SON

My son,
I send you in my only cloak

alone
upon a road I know is dark,

dangerous.
But better so. The mysteries

between us
flowered more than hearts and eyes;

thorns
grew there. Go. And do not

turn.
I would not have you wonder that

I bleed
from grasping at the thorns. I watch

you leave
shuddered in my cloak of only flesh.

MAGI, 1970

Drugged with the smell of incense,
Rounding their dull shoulders
Against two thousand years of nonsense,
Wise men come again, bent and older,
Demanding their annual share of innocence.
Each year the wind grows colder.

THE PENITENT

They went off to sin together and to love
I knew it, having heard their souls
cry out like foxes barking in the night,
having myself survived such cries.

What does it matter. They will give
each other small joys worth remembering
and an anguish consuming their small joys
and they will survive as well.

As well as I—swung from the night
like a crazy pendulum, ropes of fox bark
strung about my soul—praying their return.

PRIEST AT THE EGMONT OVERTURE

Every phrase intimates a problem, I said,
and every theme approaches resolution. No?
No, you said, and smiled. My ignorance of music
is appalling still. I noted your thin wrists.

We were home, as it turned out, at the Esplanade
but we went away to your apartment where,
sitting on the floor, we had three drinks
and sank gradually from the Boston Symphony
into each other's arms. Not love's descent,
but the use of situation: kissing your mouth
through the tangle of your scented hair,
my priest hands glancing your small breasts . . .
who would guess you had borne a child?

After a time the themes unwinding chaos
from an overture snapped in my drunken head
and I stood up, holding you away. I combed
my hair, a gesture to the neighbors, and left you.

Tonight, four years since, listening to the Egmont
I heard only our own phrases, only our themes
left tangled, unresolved on your apartment floor.

RESURRECTION

He had no eyes until the sun came up.
For years he groped the purple curtains
of the blind, hoping for a dull shadow,
a sudden color to disturb the dark.
Then there was sun.

His scorched retinas would not believe
he saw. She lay his palms upon her eyes
and waited, told him that she loved him,
drew him from the night, assured him she
had made the sun.

The world exploded in his eyes. He saw
his thirty years waiting in an open grave.
They found him dead, his cold eyes staring,
his mouth wrenched open in a terror dream
no sun could wake.

WILL AND TESTAMENT OF
A VERY PROMINENT RECLUSE

Propriety means ownership.
She wished she had it.

She had hope, creeping
in her mind the way

a dull child creeps
into the last lap

that would welcome it,
and hope sustained her.

She saw the truth
even when it hurt

because it was what was
and she preferred to see

than lose her eyes. She
looked often and saw.

She scattered dishes once,
a chairful, breaking

every one and wept
her sins until I said

we all do that.
She laughed then, frowning,

seeing that we do.
She died poor, possessor

of a bit of dignity
and several great desires.

FOOLSGOLD

Thinking he had some jewel concealed

everybody conceals something
divinity conceals its mystery

they fell on him
ransacking his tiny eyes and tearing
at the hollow underneath his ribs
they found nothing

he was the richer for it

each attack had brought him to his knees
in wonder

he walked naked among them
awkwardly at first
but in time with confidence
knowing that they saw not him
but only his thick clothes and ropes of gold

he asked for love and they gave him bread
for hope and they gave him fish
and so he died

they buried him
with speeches and a parade

in less than a year
they dug him up
thinking surely he had some jewel concealed
somewhere